ANOTHER PENGUIN SUMMER

BOOKS BY OLIN SEWALL PETTINGILL, JR.

OLIN SEWALL PETTINGILL, JR.

Another Penguin Summer

CHARLES SCRIBNER'S SONS / NEW YORK

Library of Congress Cataloging in Publication Data

Pettingill, Olin Sewall, Jr.
    Another penguin summer.

    1. Penguins—Pictorial works. 2. Birds—Falk-
land Islands—Pictorial works. I. Title.
QL696.S473P47   598.4'41'099711   75-13493
ISBN 0-684-14331-3

1 3 5 7 9 11 13 15 17 19 Q/C 20 18 16 14 12 10 8 6 4 2

PRINTED IN THE UNITED STATES OF AMERICA
Library of Congress Catalog Card Number 75-13493

ISBN 0-684-14331-3

FOR

Maurice A. E. Rumboll

PREFACE

MRS. Pettingill and I first visited the Falkland Islands in 1953–1954 to do film work for Walt Disney Productions. From the footage I obtained, the company allowed me a selection of sequences for a lecture-film that I called *Penguin Summer*. In 1960 Mrs. Pettingill published a book by the same title. When we returned to the Falklands on our own in 1971–1972 for five months, I acquired footage for a new lecture-film, *Another Penguin Summer*, and we took the pictures for this book bearing the same title.

Our photographic work would have been impossible without the hospitality and thoughtfulness of many people in the Falklands. In particular, I acknowledge with our deep appreciation: Mr. and Mrs. Roderick Napier of West Point Island; Mrs. Jack Davis and Mr. Raymond Davis of New Island; Mr. and Mrs. Alan Miller of Port San Carlos; and Mr. and Mrs. Richard Cockwell of Fox Bay East who entertained us in their homes and provided us with every means of making our stays pleasant as well as productive; Mr. Osmund Smith of Johnson's Harbour whose courtesies and accommodations made possible our work with the King Penguins at Volunteer Beach; and Mr. and Mrs. Desmond King, proprietors of the Upland Goose Hotel in Stanley where we made our headquarters, who went out of their way to ensure our comfort and facilitate our transportation to different parts of the Falklands.

Throughout this period we were especially fortunate in having the assistance of Mr. Maurice A. E. Rumboll of the Museo Argentino de Ciencias Naturales, Buenos Aires. His unfailing help, buoyant enthusiasm, and enduring companionship contributed in large measure to the success of our undertaking.

In the introduction to this book I have repeated parts of my article, "Penguins Ashore at the Falkland Islands," published in *The Living Bird* (Cornell Laboratory of Ornithology, 3rd annual, 1964, pages 45–64). For certain data on the life cycle of Rockhopper Penguins I have relied on a published study of the species at Macquarie Island by John Warham (*The Auk,* vol. 80, 1963, pages 229–256). And for certain data and information on the life cycle and behavior of King Penguins I have depended on the monographic study of the species at South Georgia by Bernard Stonehouse (*Falkland Islands Dependencies Survey,* Scientific Report no. 23, 1960).

Like my lecture-film, *Another Penguin Summer,* this book is intended to entertain as well as to inform. It will, I greatly hope, convey to people everywhere the singular charm of penguins.

OLIN SEWALL PETTINGILL, JR.

Wayne, Maine
January 1975

INTRODUCTION

FOR as long as I can remember, penguins have had a special appeal to me; more than anything else I wanted to study and photograph penguins. But I was well aware that penguins lived far away in isolated places in the Southern Hemisphere. To reach them would require a special expedition, or so I thought until I learned about the Falkland Islands. Here was a place where one could go by freighter, live with people, and be in the vicinity of several species of penguins.

The Falklands consist of two main islands and well over two hundred small islands and islets, a total land area of 4,618 square miles. The interiors of the larger islands, often hilly to ruggedly mountainous, are treeless and commonly grass-covered; their shores vary from broad sandy beaches to bold headlands with steep, sometimes perpendicular cliffs. Except in the many fiordlike harbors and narrow interchannels, the shores are almost continually pounded by surf.

In this bleak archipelago, always cool and lashed by incessant winds, 2,300 people, nearly all British or of British ancestry, make their home. Sheep-farming is the principal industry. About half the people live in Stanley, the seat of the government and only town; the others are scattered throughout the islands in some thirty settlements, the headquarters of sheep farms, at the heads of snug harbors, or on inlets well sheltered from the tumultuous sea.

We arrived in Stanley on the first of November, midspring in the Southern Hemisphere, and, in the ensuing weeks, traveled by government-operated aircraft to several settlements where we based ourselves for many days at a time near the colonies of penguins. This book of photographs shows the unique character and ways of the penguins that we observed.

Penguins—they are dual personalities. In the sea, they are the most supremely aquatic of all birds. Their sleek bodies, densely and uniformly covered with scalelike feathers, are torpedo-shaped. Their wings, reduced to strong flippers, are efficient and powerful propellers for locomotion underwater. Their short tails and stubby legs, set far back on their bodies, are steering gears. Thus equipped, penguins not only swim underwater at speeds estimated at twenty-five miles or more an hour, they also "porpoise" by alternately shooting above the surface to breathe and plunging below to swim.

On land, penguins are among the most awkward of birds. The shape of their bodies and the position of their short legs compel them either to stand upright like a man and walk with a laborious gait, or, when in a hurry, to "toboggan" by dropping on their bellies and using "all fours"—kicking with their feet and "rowing" with their flippers. Their nearsightedness, the result of a vision better suited for seeing underwater, tends to accentuate all their actions on land to the point of comedy.

Penguins undoubtedly descended from flying birds. Long, long ago in geologic time, their forebears reached the distantly isolated Antarctic region when that continent was warm. There they developed flightlessness, as have many other birds in isolated situations. But in the passing of millennia, the region became cold, glaciated, and otherwise unsuited to bird life dependent on year-round land resources. Deprived of their once-agreeable environment, these flightless birds were forced to sea, where they adapted to yet another environment. From them evolved the present-day penguins, numbering seventeen species and belonging to one family, the Spheniscidae. A few species still hug the fringe of their ancestral land, Antarctica. The others live farther north although continuing to favor the cooler waters to those warmed by equatorial currents.

The speed and agility of penguins in the sea have developed from necessity: necessity in pursuing and capturing their food, whether fish, squids, or krill—the euphausid shrimps that thrive near the surface; and necessity in escaping sea lions, leopard seals, and other aquatic predators.

Wherever they are at sea, penguins are gregarious. Each individual prefers the company of its own species, which it has no difficulty recognizing, because each species, besides having distinctive calls, has identifying marks such as a white patch on the crown, a brightly colored bill, or a crest, all conveniently on the head, the only part of a penguin visible when it is floating on water. Staying in a group has advantages. With more eyes alert, a group has a better chance than a lone individual of locating food or spotting an enemy.

Penguins are as much at home in the sea as whales and dolphins, spending months in the water, sometimes a hundred or more miles from the nearest land. But unlike these aquatic mammals, which are seabound all their lives, breeding and giving birth to their young in the water, penguins must mate, nest, rear their young, and molt on land. Thus, periodically, penguins seek the southern shores of Africa, Australia, and South America, the southern islands of the Indian, Pacific, and Atlantic oceans, and the coast of Antarctica.

When approaching the shore, penguins are cautious and hesitant, aware that in the shallow waters their principal predators, the carnivorous seals, may lurk. Should the penguins detect a seal, or as much as suspect its presence, they stay in deeper water, porpoising back and forth in a tightly knit group until, sensing that the "coast is clear," they torpedo toward the coast underwater, to explode from the surf and tumble ashore.

Once on their feet, beyond the reach of their enemies, penguins are calm and fearless. To a person approaching them slowly, they show mild concern. When rushed upon, they become alarmed and run, even toboggan, to a comfortable distance—still on the shore. Only when so frightened as to lose good sense do they return to the sea, where danger lies.

From the shore, never hurriedly, the penguins begin the trek to their traditional breeding grounds over a trail used year after year. In groups they plod, single file, stopping now and then, starting up again. The procession is altogether orderly; all participants are intent on the business of reaching their destinations.

Arriving at their breeding grounds, the penguins break ranks to play their individual roles, dictated by their sex and the stage of the nesting cycle.

The gregarious or social nature of penguins is sharply reflected by the majority of the seventeen species that breed in colonies. Though they may have abundant space—an entire island, for instance—they prefer being close together as though they needed the stimulus of an intimate association in order to breed at all. The following discussion deals only with colonial species.

Each austral spring, the penguins start reestablishing their separate colonies. A few, usually the older or more experienced birds, show up first; then gradually more follow. Among them are both sexes. Except for slight differences in size and physical proportions, the sexes look alike. And they both become vocal, equally so, with a repertoire of sounds about the same in variety. Chief among their vocalizations is the long call, loud and resonant, that in some species suggests trumpeting, in others bugling, braying, or cackling. Whatever the long call may suggest, it is distinctive of the species. Within a colony, the long call, given by one penguin after another, sounds the same, but to penguin ears it has nuances and inflections that identify both sex and individuality.

Within ten days, the colonies attain maximum size for the season. Many of the birds occupied the same colony the year before; some were born in the colonies they now occupy. All birds are immaculate in sleek, fresh plumage; all are animated and giving long calls as one bird after another advertises itself to the opposite sex. Females respond to males and males to females. Fights ensue among rivals. Here and there, apart from the fracas, two birds court each other until the other birds discover and attack them, beaks jabbing and flippers whacking. Pairs form temporarily, break up, and reform with the same or new partners. Sometimes birds renew their partnerships of the previous season. In due course, the pairs seal their partnerships by repeated copulations and settle on their territories, which are small and close together. In the case of renewed partnerships, the sites are often the ones occupied the year before. Here, for days, the members of the pairs stay close together, defending their territories against all intruders including meddlesome neighbors. Here the eggs are laid.

After laying their eggs, the females incubate them for only a few hours, then depart for the sea; whereupon the males, which have been in close attendance all the while, take over incubation. When the females return, immaculate from so many days in the water, they announce themselves with long calls from the edge of the colony. Hearing their partners respond, they hurry to them, dodging lunges and clouts from the birds they pass. Once together, the partners greet each other with mutual calls accompanied by head, flipper, and body movements. Within hours after these mutual ceremonies have subsided, the females take over incubation and the males, dirty and thin from fasting so long, head for the sea. When they return, plump and clean, again there will be greeting ceremonies and again an exchange of incubating chores. Throughout the incubation period, ranging in different species from thirty-four to sixty-four days, there may be as many as four or five exchanges.

Incubation, whether by one partner or the other, is constant and the exchange immediate—for good reason. Lurking about every colony are gulls and large gull-like birds with hawklike habits, the Great Skuas (*Catharacta skua*), ready to snatch eggs left exposed even for a few moments.

Male penguins, more frequently than their partners, are incubating the eggs when they hatch. In either case, the attending birds unceasingly cover their new chicks, giving them steady warmth, and within hours after the chicks are dry from egg moisture, begin feeding them at intervals by regurgitating partially digested food directly into their mouths. Two or three days later, the partners of the attendant birds return, initiate the customary mutual ceremonies, and take over brooding and feeding. The relieved birds soon go to sea, but not for more than a day or so. From now on the birds stay away for shorter periods and take over more often from their partners than they did during incubation, because the growing chicks require increasing amounts of food that the parents can supply only by trips to the sea.

As the chicks develop strength, balance, and use of their feet, they poke out from under their parents, spending longer periods huddled beside them. Eventually they venture away, far enough to experience attacks by neighboring adults, though rarely so far as to be beyond parental cover in case of attacks by skuas. After the chicks are about half grown and too large to be brooded, even though still down-covered, they start wandering away from their home territories and join other chicks of their age; their attending parents, now deserted, also wander from their territories without waiting for their partners to relieve them.

Until they leave the colonies, the chicks associate with one another in groups or crèches. For much of the time, the crèches are loosely formed or barely discernible. If alarmed or attacked by skuas, or if the weather turns uncomfortably cold, the chicks huddle together tightly, making the crèches very obvious.

In the early stages of crèche behavior, the chicks when hungry return to their home sites, where the parents ordinarily return to feed them. Later on, they stay with their contemporaries whether hungry or not. On hearing the long calls of their returning parents, they rush up to them, beg energetically, and are soon fed. No matter how much food they obtain, the chicks remain with their parents and harass them for more until the parents depart.

As the chicks attain full body size, they begin shedding their down, thus exposing plumage which resembles that of their elders. Fed much less frequently by the time they have lost their down, the young birds begin working their way to the sea, frequently down the trails used by their parents, going a little farther each day, but returning to the colonies when hungry to meet their parents. Once they have reached and entered the sea, accustomed themselves to the surf, and developed proficiency in swimming and diving, the time comes when they can catch their own food. Thus they become independent of their parents and no longer return to the colony.

By the time the young penguins have become independent, their parents stay in or near the colonies to molt their now badly worn and faded plumage. Since, during the molting process, their body covering is not watertight, they cannot go to sea and hence must fast for from three to four weeks until they fully acquire their new plumage.

From three to five years elapse before penguins breed. In the interval between birth and first breeding year, the sexually immature birds spend much of their time at sea, visiting each spring the vicinities of colonies where their own species breed. Here they may loiter with their contemporaries along the adjacent shore, bathing in tidal pools, sleeping, basking in the sun. Some individuals venture to the edges of the colonies as if impelled by curiosity, but few dare enter them, since they are certain to be attacked and driven out by the breeding adults.

Penguins live a long time, perhaps for twenty-five or thirty years. Nobody knows for certain.

Five species of penguins return yearly to the Falkland Islands for nesting. In greatest abundance are three: the Gentoo Penguins (*Pygoscelis papua*), standing about thirty inches tall; the Rockhopper Penguins (*Eudyptes crestatus*), about fifteen inches tall; and the Magellanic or Jackass Penguins (*Spheniscus magellanicus*), about twenty-four inches tall. The other two are the King Penguins (*Aptenodytes patagonicus*), about thirty-six inches tall, and the Macaroni Penguins (*Eudyptes chrysolophus*), as tall as the Rockhopper.

Gentoo Penguins

Gentoo Penguins are by their appearance and bearing the closest to the penguin stereotype. On level ground they walk deliberately with short strides, lifting their feet high and swaying lumberingly with each step, the head forward and flippers up and far back as a counterbalance. They can jump if they have to—across a ditch or up or down an embankment—provided the distance is no greater than twelve to fifteen inches. But before making any such jump, regardless of how often they have jumped before in the identical spot, they hesitate and inspect the situation carefully by bending forward and peering down—far down, as though they were wearing bifocal glasses—to accommodate their nearsightedness. The jump itself, once undertaken, is a matter of jerking upright, springing with both feet together, and coming down "flat-footed."

Many times we watched Gentoos arriving on a sandy beach, bound for their nesting colony. Occasionally alone, but more often in loose groups, the birds first appeared far out at sea, porpoising shoreward. When within fifty feet of the beach, and just outside the breaking waves, they dived below the surface; if we saw them at all, they were merely black streaks between waves until they burst out of the surf, a foot or more clear of the water, and landed on the beach, sometimes upright, sometimes on their bellies, now and then tumbling and somersaulting. They recovered their composure quickly and hurried—tobogganing at times—up the beach above the tideline, where they invariably stopped to rest with other Gentoos recently arrived.

At one place we watched Gentoos landing on a ledge shelf that rose four or five feet straight up from the sea. Just before reaching it the porpoising birds disappeared momentarily below the surface; there, gathering momentum, they vaulted clear of the water in the direction of the ledge. Some, misjudging the height, struck the perpendicular face of the ledge and fell back into the water; the others made the top—with variable results. Coming down on the smooth wet ledge feet first, they slipped and skidded on their backs, sides, or bellies, sometimes sliding into and upsetting another bird that had just gotten on its feet. Rare was the penguin that landed upright and stayed that way.

The rest period after coming ashore lasted for a few minutes to half an hour, or even longer. Nearly always the birds preened; some of them slumped, sleeping on their feet, and a few lay down on their bellies and slept soundly. In general, the birds were docile and showed little if any hostility toward one another although each bird was careful to keep its "individual distance." Once in a while a bird trumpeted—gave a long call, which in the Gentoos is loud and resonant like the blast of a trumpet.

The landing marks only one stage in the return to the colony, for the trail ahead is long, often a mile or more, over bluffs, through valleys, and across streams, and eventually up a hill to the site of the colony, overlooking the sea. We knew of one colony on the summit of a 600-foot hill. Why should Gentoos select such high ground for their colonies when there are places so much nearer the sea that would require far less effort? The only reasonable answer, based purely on speculation, is that the species clings to an ancestral habit of nesting on bare ridges between ice-filled valleys when the area was glaciated. For heavy-bodied birds on short legs, the climb meant a considerable expenditure of energy. No wonder the Gentoos needed a rest period beforehand.

Generally the rest period was terminated by one bird, usually one of the last birds to arrive from the sea and disinclined to linger. Passing through the slumbering group toward the trail and perhaps stopping to trumpet once as though sounding reveille, it soon picked up a following of aroused birds, each falling into single file and more or less the same distance apart.

The birds on the trail were wary of us, never letting us come close to them. At the same time, they were reluctant to leave the trail, running up and down it, depending on the direction of our approach. When we deliberately blocked their passage, the birds left the trail helter-skelter in all directions, running and tobogganing in complete disarray. As soon as we moved away, the birds came back at once and continued in the direction they were going in the first place. The Gentoos seemed to know only one way to reach the colony and that was by the trail. Away from it they became bewildered and confused.

When Gentoos plodding up the trail met groups coming from the colony, there was no concern, no problem. The trail was wide enough to permit passing right or left without touching. Stops on the trail were frequent, the birds standing quietly—and panting if the day was warm. If, while one group rested, another caught up, the arrival of the second group often started the first moving again. Rarely did one group overtake and pass another.

The Gentoos did not travel on the trail at night, but all during the day groups paraded up or down at intervals, except in the first hours of the morning, when many groups went down, and in the last daylight hours, when many groups went up. At such times, the groups followed one another so closely that the trail often looked like a long string of black-and-white beads across the gray hillside.

The colonies of Gentoos, always on level or gently sloping ground, may contain anywhere from several to hundreds of pairs. Regardless of the colony's size or the space available, the pairs place their nests close together with just enough distance apart to prevent birds sitting on nests from reaching over and poking one another. This extreme proximity proves troublesome for the birds whose nests are deep in the colonies. To reach their nests they have to "run the gauntlet" by maneuvering the narrow passages between nests while receiving on both sides jabs in the ribs from the nest occupants which are intent on guarding their territory.

The nests are simply bowls, consisting of twigs from the diddle-dee, a common shrub, and grasses and assorted debris. Most of this material the male gathers while his partner, in the middle of the nest site, arranges some of it around her and tramples and presses down the rest of it beneath her to make the nest deep enough to hold the eggs and fit the shape of her body.

For the nests being built on the edge of the colony, the males readily find twigs and grasses outside. But for the nest being built within the colony, the males enjoy no such luxury. To obtain materials, they could—and sometimes do—go outside the colony, but this means running the gauntlet twice, out and back. Instead, they resort to the much less painful and certainly the more convenient procedure of filching material from neighboring nests. This requires stealth conditioned by experience.

Typically, the male bent on thievery wanders between nests, always slowly and unobtrusively so as not to arouse the ire of the occupants, meanwhile watching carefully for just the right opportunity: the well-furnished nest whose occupant is asleep or looking the other way. At last, spotting it, he sneaks up near enough and no more, grabs a mouthful, and retreats instantly before the surprised owner can retaliate. Depositing the loot at the side of his partner on the nest, he is soon on the prowl again—in another direction.

Gentoos normally produce a clutch of two eggs, which both sexes incubate until they hatch after forty to forty-one days. When the pair changes over at the nest, the relieved partner, in no hurry, loiters close by, stretching and preening. If the relieved bird is a male, more than likely he goes about gathering—stealing if need be—more material for the nest, a persisting trait albeit a waste of time now that the nest is made. Before long, the relieved partner, whether male or female, starts the long walk down to the sea, where it may spend several days feeding and building up fat reserves.

The two down-covered chicks, born at about the same time, are able to walk away from the nest when six weeks old—leaving their guarding parents or the parents leaving them, whichever the case may be—and join their contemporaries in the crèches. After about twelve weeks they have lost most of their down and, practically full grown, begin venturing down the trails to the sea. During this long period, both parents feed them but with decreasing frequency. When the youngsters attain the crèche stage, only one or the other of the parents returns from the sea with food for them, usually in the late afternoon. Mealtime is the big event, the climax of the day.

Through the morning, youngsters in the crèche stage are generally inactive, many sleeping flat out on their bellies, flippers outstretched, feet sticking out back with soles up. By noon, they are awake and lively. They chase one another in a kind of play, examine sticks, broken eggshells, or other objects that catch their eye, sometimes picking them up and running about with them, and they exercise by jumping up and down, fanning their flippers, and scampering in short circles. By midafternoon, their appetites enormous, they focus attention on the trail ends for the return of their parents.

On arriving, each parent trumpets. Whereupon its own chick, or chicks, respond by rushing up, giving juvenile calls, and begging—nibbling at the parent's bill to induce the delivery of food. The parent soon obliges with several feedings until, the store of food in its gullet exhausted, it has no more to deliver. The youngster, not satisfied, continues begging. The parent pecks the youngster with the obvious implication "Quit it"; the youngster fails to heed. Finally, annoyed beyond endurance, the parent turns and runs away with the youngster in pursuit, through the colony and around the colony, stumbling over empty nests, bumping into other birds, the youngster keeping up with the parent even to the extent of occasionally stepping on its tail. Now and then the parent stops, the youngster resumes begging, and the food chase begins again. And so on. The whole performance, so comical because neither adult nor offspring is fleet-footed, ordinarily ends when the youngster falls down and gets hopelessly behind or, its stomach full from already generous feedings, it cannot keep the pace.

The parent penguin, in feeding its chicks, often must cope with another problem, the Dolphin Gulls (*Leucophaeus scoresbii*). Opportunists that these gulls are, on seeing a penguin regurgitating food, they swoop down and harass the bird, causing it to drop on the ground some of the food that was on its way into the mouths of the chicks. Annoyed and distracted, the penguin tries to strike at the gulls and loses more food. Having received just what they wanted, the gulls attack all the more vigorously, obtaining more food and confusing the penguin until finally it is nearly a nervous wreck.

Rockhopper Penguins

Rockhopper Penguins are not only smaller than Gentoos but livelier and more agile in all their actions. As their name implies, they have, besides a forward-walking gait, a method of progression by jumps, with feet together, which one ornithologist likened to a man in a sack race. No doubt such locomotion, coupled with sharp nails on their toes, is an adaptation for maneuvering over rocks and abrupt, rocky inclines. Certainly, on level ground, hopping has no advantage over walking. We have movies showing Rockhoppers hopping and walking side by side with no difference in forward speed.

Our principal observations on Rockhoppers were made at New Island, where some 100,000 pairs nest in a colony on the upper slopes of several rock-strewn bluffs, two hundred to three hundred feet above the sea. Below the colony and between it and the sea are perpendicular cliffs, cutting off access from the sea except through steep ravines.

The landing places for the Rockhoppers in this colony are several jagged ledges and gigantic slabs of rock that tip sharply into the sea, like ramps. No spot can be considered a beach. On the ramps, below the high-tide mark, are mats of thick, stringy kelp. Against these landing places, the sea, constantly whipped by the ever-prevalent westerly winds, often at gale force, surges and crashes, sending up great geysers of spray. The swells, however, are never mountainous enough to prohibit the Rockhoppers from coming ashore or departing.

The Rockhoppers were consistently gregarious in all their actions and never more so than when coming to land. Repeatedly, we watched a tightly knit group offshore porpoising toward a favorite ramp. And then, on the crest of a breaking wave or in front of it, they shot as high as four feet clear of the water, flippers beating the air, and plopped on the ledge, feet first if they were lucky but more often on their bellies. Recovering instantly, they started hopping like so many jumping beans to reach the high ground before the next breaker. Almost invariably, a few birds mismanaged their landing by getting entangled in the kelp, by failing to jump clear of the water, or by not getting far enough up the ramp. Consequently, they were soon at the mercy of the next breaker and, overwhelmed under an avalanche of white water, were pulled by the undertow back into the sea. But no matter, they eventually emerged on the back side of the spent wave and renewed their struggle toward the ramp. Rockhoppers, we realized, are no more troubled by tempestuous surf than flying birds by raging winds.

Once on the ledges above the surf, the Rockhoppers rested briefly, shaking the water from their heads, flippers, and tails and preening. Then the procession to and up the ravines began. As the trails narrowed, the birds moved in single file.

Both trails pass over hard, sedimentary ledges and loose rocks whose upper faces are often tilted at a near-perpendicular angle and have deep vertical scars or grooves formed by the nails of the Rockhoppers, no doubt by the yearly passage of millions of them over many centuries.

Watching the Rockhoppers climb these ledges, we noticed that they used their slightly hooked bills as well as their nails for holding on to the surface when it became excessively steep. We observed too that they could climb more effectively by hopping than by walking, gaining as much as ten to twelve inches per hop—provided that their nails were firmly in the grooves so as to prevent them from slipping backward.

The birds were not especially wary of us if we sat quietly or moved slowly. Almost at our feet they went by unconcernedly, intent on climbing, which required great effort. In the sheltered ravines any appreciable sunlight caused them to breathe audibly, even pant, and to sneeze frequently, clearing the rapidly accumulating moisture in their nasal passages. If we intentionally disturbed them by coming down the path quickly from above, they panicked instantly—jumping, slipping, and tumbling down the trail in a general pileup that soon blocked passage of the birds coming from behind. As soon as we drew back up the trail or sat still, the procession began as if nothing had happened.

The trip down the trail involved considerable jumping from step down to step. Where the birds had to climb by bill and nail when making their ascent, they frequently stood sideways and slid down on their feet, one foot in advance of the other while keeping the body upright.

Once down the trail and on the landing rock, the Rockhoppers chose to go to sea by different ways, depending on the state of the surf. If the waves were running high, they walked out onto the rocks or ledges that rose straight above the surf, sometimes as high as ten feet. From here they jumped either feetfirst or, less commonly, headfirst. The act of plunging was almost always preceded by long periods of hesitancy during which the birds went to the edge, looked down, stepped back, rested, looked down again, and so on. At long last, one bird dropped off and the others followed en masse. By contrast, if the surf was moderate, the Rockhoppers went to the landing ramps and ran down into the water, a feat they could not accomplish when the waves were mountainous, since it would have been difficult to enter the water without being swept back up the ramp.

The broad shelf below the cliffs was a loitering area for many Rockhoppers. Some were obviously yearling birds; others may have been older birds, "unemployed" during the current nesting season. Where there were depressions in the ledge shelf, water collected after rains or high tides. In these pools the loiterers bathed together, splashing water over themselves with their flippers, diving as deeply as the pools would permit, and now and then playfully chasing one another. Certain individuals ran into the pools and swam across, splashing all the way, then returned—seemingly for no other reason than to enjoy themselves.

Like Gentoo Penguins, Rockhoppers are colonial nesters, but their choice of sites always involves rugged situations—outcropping rocks and ledges on the steep declivities of bluffs high above the sea. The site of the great colony at New Island is characteristic.

When we first approached the New Island colony from the interior, we heard it long before we climbed the bluffs and looked down their sides toward the sea. Rockhoppers are the noisiest of penguins, and we first saw them at the start of the nesting season, when they were their very noisiest. The colony sounded like an enormous chicken coop with all the occupants cackling at once.

The nests were between rocks or on the flat shelves of ledges, anywhere that could accommodate their simple bowls of tussock grass, which fringed the colony. Many nests were close together, uncomfortably so, we discovered when we walked between them. Lacking the gentleness of the Gentoos, which retreated just a few feet from their nests when we stepped between them, the Rockhoppers stayed on their nests with defiance, facing us, crests erected, cheek feathers puffed out, and mouths open, threatening attack. And attack some of them did, grabbing a leg and pounding furiously with both flippers. If one latched on above a boot, its pinch—bite is a better term—was certain to draw blood and leave a scar.

In getting to their own nests after coming up the ravine from the sea, Rockhoppers have a dual problem: to maneuver over and among all the rocks and ledges and at the same time to avoid attacks of the birds on the nests they must pass. Their solution is to hop from one safe rock to another whenever possible, keeping their heads down to see where their feet are going, then halting every so often to stand erect and look about just to make sure they are moving in the right direction. When they must pass through an area crowded with nests, or should they slip off a rock into a crowded area, they put their heads down, sleek their feathers to make themselves as thin as possible, hold their flippers in front of them, and hop with all possible speed to minimize the bites and poundings from both sides.

The incessant, almost deafening cacophony of the Rockhopper colony early in the nesting season is best explained this way. A bird returning from the sea to relieve its incubating partner stops a short distance in front of the nest and gives the long call that in the Rockhopper Penguin is a loud, raucous, somewhat grating cackle, delivered with the head up and shaking and the bill open and pointed skyward. The partner on the nest may or may not respond, but many other neighboring birds do, starting a wave of cackling that practically sweeps the colony. Then comes the mutual display when the relieving bird and its partner, now together at the nest and standing chest to chest, both lift their heads vertically and, shaking them with mouths agape, cackle at the top of their lungs. This triggers more cackling among the neighbors. The same birds repeat the display at least two or three times with the resulting echoes beyond. Considering that there are thousands of Rockhoppers in the colony, with nesting birds by the score being relieved at the same time, one can understand why cotton is recommended for the ears of human visitors.

Rockhoppers usually lay two eggs. As soon as the female produces the second one, the larger, she begins incubating them. The male relieves her now and then until the eggs hatch about thirty-four days later. The chicks, sixteen or more days after birth, gather in crèches, but before they do, the male broods and guards them while the female supplies the food. Mealtime, as in the Gentoo colonies, is in the late afternoon. The returning parents go directly to their old nests. Sometimes the youngsters are already there, waiting anxiously, having left the crèches in anticipation of their parents' arrival. If not, the parents' cackles, summoning their offspring, bring them in a hurry, peeping and with flippers waving. More often than not, youngsters other than their own similarly respond, but a few effective jabs from the parents make the point: "No food for strangers." Full grown, after about nine weeks, the youngsters depart for the sea.

The Rockhoppers are not alone in their colony. Long before they establish it in the spring, Black-browed Albatrosses (*Diomedea melanophrys*)—huge, lordly birds with wings spreading seven feet—reclaim their conelike nests of mud scattered here and there in the colony site, lay their single eggs, and begin incubating them. With the arrival of the Rockhoppers come the handsome King Cormorants (*Phalacrocorax albiventer*) to reoccupy their colonial enclaves within the penguin aggregation. Since both the albatrosses and cormorants reach and leave their nests by air, they rarely conflict with the grounded Rockhoppers and consequently are ignored.

Constantly patrolling the Rockhopper colony from the air or standing on an overlooking boulder or crag are the Great Skuas, ever watchful

24

for an exposed clutch of eggs or vulnerable chicks—chicks straying too far from the protection of their parents or crèches, or chicks that have been maimed by resentful neighbors into whose territories they wandered. Many skuas nest near the colonies, convenient to their principal source of food when they are rearing their own young.

After the Rockhoppers have left the colony, and the King Cormorants too at about the same time, the site suggests a circus ground the day after the tents have been struck and the show has left town. Young albatrosses, slower to develop independence than penguins or cormorants, look forsaken on their nest cones, never uttering a sound except when their parents sail down to feed them. The only activity is provided by the skuas searching the site and squabbling and croaking over the remaining chick carcasses or anything else still edible. Otherwise the site is stone quiet—blissfully so.

Magellanic or Jackass Penguins

The Magellanic Penguins we preferred to call Jackass Penguins as the Falkland people do. It is a more appropriate name, as I shall explain, as well as more manageable. In using it I am mindful of the South African species (*Spheniscus demersus*) bearing the same English name.

Intermediate in size between the Gentoos and Rockhoppers, the Jackass Penguins are no less distinctive in locomotion on land. Like the Gentoos, they walk with high, short steps but sway only slightly from side to side; as they step forward, they keep their flippers either at the side or a bit forward. They are more agile than the Gentoos, less so than Rockhoppers. When tobogganing they proceed speedily by running on the tips of their toes and flippers, bellies clear of the ground.

Besides their manner of locomotion, another distinctive action of Jackass Penguins, shared by all members of their genus, is that of cocking and turning the head from side to side, peering first out of one eye and then the other at any object immediately in front. It is as though the birds cannot believe what they see out of one eye and have to look with the other eye just to make sure.

We found Jackass Penguins similar to Gentoos in coming from and returning to the sea. They landed mainly on beaches and seldom attempted to maneuver over rugged terrain.

Jackass Penguins nest in burrows and show little tendency to colonize—that is, to nest close together and to participate in concerted activities. At New Island, we noted some pairs occupying burrows, generally widely spaced, in the same peat-covered hillsides and others entirely by themselves in their own peat banks. On some of the smaller islands covered with tussock, pairs had burrows under the hummocks at widely separated spots.

Jackass Penguins dig their own burrows, or reoccupy burrows that the species excavated the previous year, in slopes overlooking the sea, and go to and from the water by the most direct route, which during the course of the nesting season becomes a well-worn path. Sometimes a pair has its own private path all the way to the beach. More often the paths of several pairs converge into one as they near the beach.

Trips over the paths are more often by individuals walking alone than by groups. There is no time of day when their movements are more evident, although we surmised that they, like the Gentoos and Rockhoppers, go to and return from the sea more commonly in the early morning and the late afternoon.

The Jackass Penguins were more wary of us when we came upon them away from the water and the shore than the Gentoos and Rockhoppers were. No matter how slowly we approached, they almost always increased their speed, sometimes running or tobogganing away from us. But there were exceptions, such as when we stood in their path. We could not deter them—and I received bruises on my shin when I thought I could. One day, walking up to a Jackass Penguin proceeding down its path over a grassy slope to the sea, I found myself three feet from the bird, determined not to budge, not to step aside. Then in an instant, to my complete surprise, it reached out and grabbed the top of my boot with its sharply hooked bill and pummeled my leg with the full force of its flippers. Kicked off, it attacked again and again. It was I who ultimately stepped aside—and gladly.

This experience gave us a special respect for the Jackass Penguins we met on the narrow paths through the thick tussock grass. We always stepped aside to let them pass, and they always did, with dignity and unconcern.

Arriving at the entrances to their burrows, the Jackass Penguins give their long calls, like the brays of jackasses, and hence their English name. Preliminary to the bray itself, each performer begins heaving as though it were going to be sick. Then lifting its head vertically and opening its mouth, it lets forth a series of woeful yells, each one accomplished by swelling and collapsing the chest to take in and expel the air. The yells, half a dozen or so, decrease in volume as the head finally comes down, and the display terminates with a few hiccups. The brayings of the Jackass Penguins, while signaling their arrivals at the burrows, are given under other circumstances throughout the breeding season, day or night. Woeful hardly describes the sounds in the distance, on a dark, windy night. To me they were hair-raising, the awful calls one might hear from a person suffering his final agonies or being gruesomely murdered.

To a chamber, deep in their burrows, the birds carry grasses for their nests. Here they lay two eggs. We could not determine how long they incubated the eggs before they hatched, nor could we follow the early development of the chicks, which both parents feed and brood. After the chicks are about half grown, they emerge from the burrows, spending much time on the "doorsteps" sleeping, basking in the sun, and receiving attention from their parents. At the slightest disturbance, they retreat into the burrows out of sight—and their parents too, if present—but curiosity prevents them from staying long. They soon come poking out to see what is going on.

The young birds eventually collect in groups. On a sunny day at the end of the nesting season we watched a large group of about 150 fully grown youngsters on a broad beach. Much of the time they huddled together in a tight pack without regard to individual distance. At intervals, a few left to enter the slight surf and were sent sprawling by a breaker. Some of them, after gaining confidence, proceeded to bathe by dipping forward and bringing water over their backs or by rolling over on their backs. All the while their flippers and feet kept the water splashing and boiling. The day was not far off when they would be at home in the sea.

King Penguins

King Penguins are the most colorful of the world's penguins and second only in size to the Emperor Penguins of the Antarctic. They walk with great dignity, straight upright, with a pendulum swing of the head, their exceptionally long flippers held out and down. Their stubby tails with strong, two-inch-long quills serve as a brush and a prop—a brush for sweeping away anything in back and a prop enabling them to sit back and relax on their "heels," toes up. When sleeping, they may simply slump while still standing and tuck the bill under a flipper just as their flying ancestors tucked the bill under a wing, or they may lie down on their bellies flat out, feet extended back with soles up.

While not among the noisiest of penguins, Kings can be vociferous when the need arises. Their long call is loud and vibrant, though slightly muffled, and distinctly buglelike. Before uttering it, the bird stands bolt upright, back arched, abdomen drawn in, flippers close to the body, and bill forward. Then, after slowly stretching the neck up to the limit and pointing the bill skyward—but keeping it closed—the bird makes its volley of bugle notes as the chest expands and contracts in rhythm. With the last note sounded, the bird snaps the bill back to forward position and stands motionless a few seconds as if judging the effect of the performance on its fellows.

Though gathering in tightly packed colonies for breeding, King Penguins have no nests, only breeding sites, each one little more than two or three feet in diameter. On this site the female lays her single egg for the season and, with her bill, rolls it up on the top of her feet. Then she slumps so that the egg is covered by a fold in the skin of her lower abdomen and proceeds to incubate it. She sits in a hunched upright position—not down as do the Gentoo and Rockhopper Penguins—and the skin of her lower abdomen bulges forward covering her feet. If she dislikes where she is sitting, she moves, the egg still in position, by hitching one foot ahead of the other at a pace as imperceptible as a snail's. The male stays with her, lashing out and clouting intrusive neighbors until, within a few hours, she turns the egg over to him by standing up and letting it roll off her feet. She soon heads for the sea, where she may spend two or three weeks. During the fifty-four days from the time the egg is laid until it hatches, the partners relieve each other four times. The female takes over at the last exchange and covers the egg until the chick is born.

At birth the chick is frail and practically naked with only wisps of short down. Needing constant warmth for the next few days, it stays under its warm cover, its wobbly head appearing only when it is hungry. In feeding the chick, which has been whistling faintly for its meal, the parent bends down and, opening the bill, lets the chick reach into the mouth to take what is regurgitated.

Both parents feed the chick and take turns brooding. After a week or so the chick begins spending more and more time outside the skinfold, resting against the parent, and before long taking steps away. As it gets larger and develops a thick covering of down, it outgrows the protection of the skinfold. By the time it is four weeks old, the best it can do, when frightened, is to run to the parent and push its head and shoulders out of sight. At five weeks of age, the chick begins mingling with its contemporaries and in another week joins them in crèches. Its down has become thick and long, so furry as to give the youngster the appearance of a teddy bear. The chick continues growing for the next five weeks until, at twelve weeks of age, it is as large as its parents—but still down-covered. Indeed, it is so heavily covered that it looks larger than its parents!

Though full grown, the young bird stays down-covered and dependent on its parents for the next twenty-eight weeks—until it is at least ten months old. Further development has virtually stalled. Fed infrequently by its parents, it loses weight. Finally, after about the age of ten months, it is fed more often, regains weight, sheds its down, and leaves for the sea and independence.

After the young bird departs for the sea, the parents stay ashore near the colony and molt, a process that takes about a month. Not long thereafter they breed again, but it will be later in the year than when they bred previously, because their chick took so long to develop independence. As a result, the next chick they produce will be later in leaving for the sea—

so late that the pair will not raise a third chick within a three-year period. King Penguins are exceptional among birds in producing young twice in three years instead of annually as most birds do.

King Penguins are reputed to have been common in the Falklands until the sealers and whalers in the eighteenth and early nineteenth centuries slaughtered them for their oil. By the turn of this century, they were totally extirpated, or at least so rare that the sight of a single bird was a record of note. Now, ever so gradually, pairs of King Penguins are breeding in the Falklands, usually in or near the colonies of Gentoo Penguins, which seem to act as decoys. We were delighted to find, on our recent return to the Falklands, that a small colony of Kings has become well established back from Volunteer Beach on the periphery of a thriving colony of some two hundred pairs of Gentoos.

We first visited the colony of King Penguins early in December. In a cluster were about thirty adults, some courting and others incubating. Scattered around the edge of the colony were nine huge teddy-bear chicks and, some distance away, a group of ten molting adults sitting hunched and disconsolate on a patch of ground white with the feathers they had already shed. The overall situation was quite unlike the one in the neighboring Gentoo colony, where all the birds in evidence were adults attending their eggs or newly hatched chicks.

King Penguins, we noted, are gentle and sedate, rarely given to hurried or ungraceful movements. When we approached the adults in the colony, they showed only mild concern, those on the edge stepping away without losing their composure or showing hostility. If we stood quietly, they approached us with cautious interest. If we were so forward as to touch them, we were rewarded for our impudence with a thrust from the bill and a couple of flipper slaps for emphasis.

We watched one adult arriving from the sea. A short distance from the colony, it stopped and bugled. Instantly, four teddy-bear chicks converged on it, whistling loudly and begging. They were as tall as the adult bird, practically overwhelming it in their anxiety, but the adult soon discouraged them with effective jabs and bugled again. This time three adults came forward—a welcoming committee of sorts—and faced the newcomer.

All four bugled in turn with intervening moments of silence; then all of them paraded to the colony in single file, the newcomer drawing up in the rear.

Then an adult that we had failed to notice at first on the edge of the colony suddenly bugled. No doubt a male, he soon attracted another bird, probably a female. As she approached, he turned his head from side to side, flashing his orange ear patches for her benefit. She responded by flashing hers. Inspired by the attention, he arched his back, pushed out his chest, and began to strut, bill forward and head swaying far to one side and then the other. She assumed the same posture, swaying like a pendulum too, and followed him around the colony. The whole performance was an early stage in courtship—perhaps the getting-acquainted stage.

Within the colony we noted a male and female which had selected a breeding site and were in the later stages of courting. Facing each other and almost touching, they extended their necks as high as they could, pointed their bills skyward, and swayed their heads. They made no sounds. Then, still facing each other, one bird lowered its head and began opening and closing the bill rapidly, making a rattling sound, sometimes nibbling at an object on the ground or the partner's plumage as though preening. The partner responded with similar actions. Later the male arched his neck over hers and nibbled her gently. Eventually he mounted her and copulation followed.

When we returned in early February to the colony of King Penguins, we counted twenty-two adults. Four were attending small chicks and seven had eggs; they were all close together. Most of the time, they were quiet, sleeping. But now and then, for no apparent reason, one bird poked at another, triggering a bout of hostile interaction, every bird lashing at another and grunting as it did so. Soon they were quiet again and started to doze.

Nowhere were there any teddy-bear chicks. It would be three months, in May (late fall), before the generation of chicks, now newly hatched in the colony, would be in the teddy-bear stage, and early November (midspring) before they would go to sea. By then another group of adults would have started breeding. The site of a King Penguin colony is never deserted. This is not the case with the other species of penguins.

Moments later the Gentoos exploded from the surf. Though most of them landed on their feet, some came down on their bellies and a few even turned somersaults, but they quickly recovered, picking themselves up and pattering hurriedly up the beach to avoid the next breaker.

RIGHT

The Gentoo Penguin conforms to the traditional penguin image: humanlike posture, heavy set and rather portly, calm in attitude, deliberate in manner, and formal in black-and-white attire with an image-defying dash of bright color—orange, red, or pink—on the bill and feet.

OPPOSITE

All day, every day throughout the nesting season, the Gentoos came ashore, sometimes in twos and threes, but usually in large groups. Rarely was a bird ever alone. Heavy surf and blowing sand they ignored.

After coming ashore and resting briefly to recoup their energies, the Gentoos in groups begin the trek overland to the nesting colonies. Strung out in single file, they follow ancestral trails that may take them a mile or more through valleys, up hills, and across ridges.

We stood quietly on one trail and watched Gentoos coming toward us like so many walking laundry bags. They were so busy looking down to see where their feet were going that they did not notice us until they drew close. Breaking out of single file, they stopped stone-still and stared. Birds coming along behind them stopped. Traffic kept piling up until one unconcerned bird coming from behind detoured around us, never stopping. The others then fell into line and followed.

The Gentoos returning to one colony broke tradition by coming ashore on a high, flat-topped, sheer-sided ledge instead of on a beach. Shooting out of the sea to reach the top, some of them made it the first time. Others failed—not leaping high enough, they hit the sheer side and fell back into the sea—and had to try again in hopes of better luck. Once the Gentoos made the top, they almost invariably slipped and skidded on the water-glazed surface.

All penguins, like this Gentoo, are seabirds, admirably suited and equipped for swimming with flippers for propellers, feet and tail for rudders. With feet far back on the body, all penguins are less suited for walking on land, to which they must come for nesting. They have to assume an upright stance because there is no other way they can balance themselves. Being short-legged, too, and heavy-bodied, penguins have to walk with short, quick steps and rock the body from side to side, or waddle, in order to make any progress. Pity this poor Gentoo, which has to climb a long hill.

The Gentoo trails present numerous hazards—rocky outcrops, peat slips, ponds, and streams. Here two birds inspect a streamlet across the path, seemingly at a loss to decide whether to jump over it or wade through it. Although seabirds, spending much of their time in the water, penguins once on land seem reluctant to get their feet wet.

Gentoos use the trails all day although the traffic is heavier in the early morning and the afternoon. Toward evening, as here, the traffic begins tapering off. At night, movement on the trails ceases altogether.

A Gentoo Penguin colony shows up clearly, a circle of white against the bleak, treeless Falkland terrain. The penguins establish a colony in the same general area year after year, but they usually select a fresh plot within the area where there will be a new supply of nesting material.

Rockhopper Penguins are aptly named. They come ashore on rocks; they loiter on rocks; they place their nests on rocks; and, although they can walk perfectly well, they often—especially when they are in a hurry—put both feet together and hop on rocks.

All penguins are white below, black above, with the distinguishing features on the head. The Rockhopper Penguin has a streak of yellow feathers above each eye ending in a tuft above each ear. The bill is red, matching the eye.

When the Rockhopper sits quietly, resting and surveying the sea from its high perch, the feathers on its head are sleek and smooth and the tufts of yellow feathers hang down like tassels. When the same bird is disturbed or its ire aroused, the black feathers on its head stand straight up and the yellow tufts stick way out, turning the small, placid penguin into a ferocious, 15-inch-high monster.

For their nesting colonies Rockhopper Penguins prefer rugged situations on an ocean-facing coast. One of their largest colonies is here at New Island on the brows of the great cliffs towering above the open Atlantic.

Thousands of Rockhoppers come ashore hourly on the way to the great colony at New Island. We watched them landing on one of the ledges that slanted into the sea, forming a ramp. While hundreds were coming up the ramp toward us, many others were on their way in to the ramp as far out in the surf as we could see. Surf was no more problem for them than wind is a problem for flying birds.

The flippers of penguins are operated by muscles of enormous strength, enabling them to leap far out of the water without using their feet. Here, jumping out of the surf onto the ramp, the Rockhoppers almost seem to be flying. After they come down, they begin hopping up the ramp through the mat of loose kelp growing at the sea's edge. If they become entangled in the kelp, as is often the case, the next breaker crashes over them and washes them out.

The climb begins from a ramp to the colony above the cliffs. Here the ascent is gradual, the going easy. Some of the birds hop, others walk, yet the birds hopping make no better progress than the birds walking.

OVERLEAF

As shown in these two views, the Rockhoppers, in order to reach the colony, will ascend by one of two routes. Some will follow the short route (left) up the precipitous ravine, a veritable chimney, to the colony, a part of which shows at the top of the path. The others will follow the much longer, more gradual route (right) winding up to the colony, out of view on the right. Like a highway leading out of a big city, this route branches and rebranches and the traffic becomes dispersed.

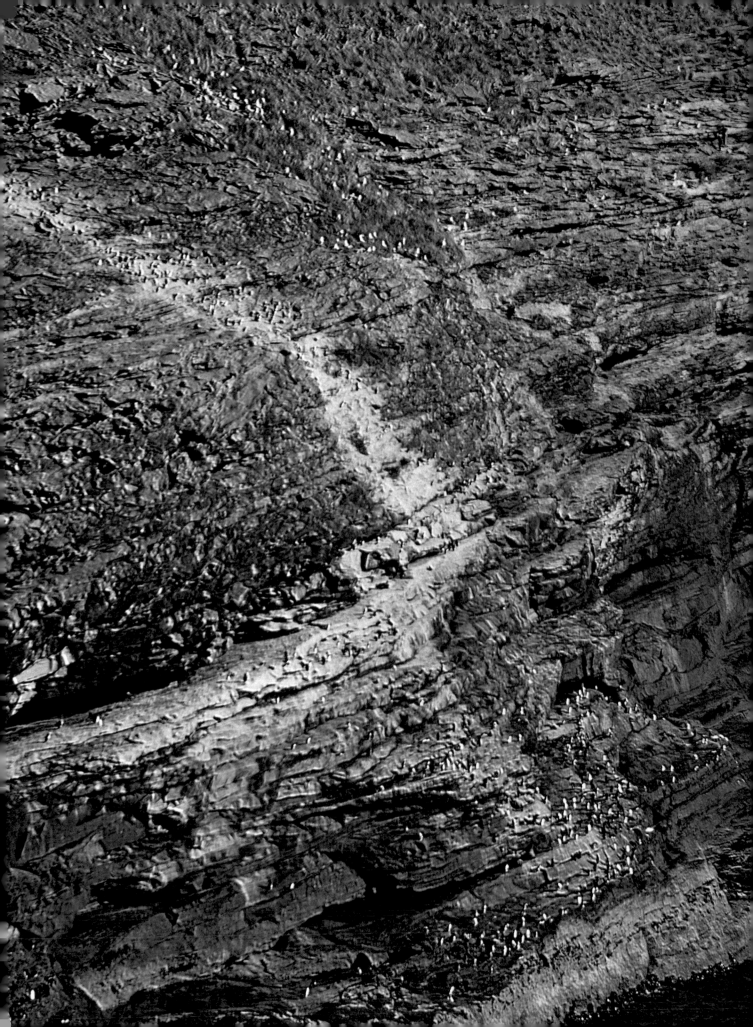

Frequently the Rockhoppers must scramble up rock faces on all fours with the bill for a grip. The sharp claws on their toes secure good footholds.

OPPOSITE
Rock climbing. When possible, the Rockhoppers jump from one ledge up to the next. If they misjudge the distance or slip, they may fall head over heels to the bottom of the sharp rise. No matter. Sturdily built and chunky, with tough skins and a thick, cushioning layer of fat beneath, they pick themselves up, shake their heads, get their bearings, and begin again.

A close look at one of the rocks in a steep trail up which countless Rockhoppers make their way to the colony. Note the parallel grooves they have scratched with their claws. One wonders how many birds it has taken over how many years to scratch the rocks as deeply as this rock.

We stood on the edge of one Gentoo colony, looking toward the sea, entranced as we always were by the sweeping view, the openness of the Falklands—the bay and the hill on the far shore, the little patch of Gentoos standing just above the landing rock, and more of the black-and-white birds plodding upward toward us. Although the grade of the hill was more gentle than most, it was a long, arduous climb for the heavy-bodied birds on their short legs and rest stops were many. If the sun was out and the day the least bit warm, some of the penguins actually panted.

The Gentoos nest close together, yet not too close. They place their nests just far enough apart so that a penguin sitting on one nest cannot quite reach and interfere with a penguin on another. This arrangement is hard on any penguin that must walk between nests to get to its own. Usually it has to "run the gauntlet" of pokes and jabs all along the way.

A Gentoo lays two eggs each season and the female and male take turns incubating them. One or the other is always on the nest, ready to defend the contents against the Dolphin Gulls and Great Skuas that patrol all the penguin colonies, looking for a meal. Against a man, these gentle penguins have no defense. They quietly step aside.

Gentoo Penguins incubate their eggs by sitting on them just like chickens. While one bird is on the nest, the other is at sea feeding, dozing on its feet beside its incubating partner, or, if the male, meandering about the colony searching for nesting material. Though the simple nest is already built as well as it needs to be, the male keeps adding grasses and twigs for days after the eggs have hatched.

This male Gentoo Penguin returns to his nest with a mouthful of turf that he will dump beside or on the back of his partner. Possibly he gathered the material outside the colony, although more than likely he stole it from a nearby nest.

The King Penguin, the most colorful of all penguins, has an orange bill tipped with black; a silvery gray to steel blue back; a jet black head and throat; and orange ear patches narrowing and joining under the throat a band of equally brilliant orange that blends downward to gold, then yellow, and finally shining white on the midbreast and abdomen. The bird in this picture stands in a sort of slump, a posture that Kings may assume for hours. Its huge feet point up; its weight rests on the "heels" and stiff tail.

Colorful as it is, the King Penguin lacks "facial expression" because the contrast between the dark brown eye and uniformly black head is so slight. A short distance away one has trouble determining just where the eye is and whether the bird is awake or asleep.

BELOW

The one King Penguin colony in the Falklands, a small one, was beside a small brook on a lush green flat, below and a little apart from a large Gentoo colony. Although the Gentoos' trail to the sea passed close to the King Penguins' domain, we noticed no contact between the two colonies. The Kings ignored the Gentoos' winding trail and had their own route straight to the sea.

King Penguins, exceedingly tame and seemingly gentle, have an unbounded curiosity, particularly about anything or anyone they have not seen before. This King Penguin, on discovering Maurice near the edge of the colony, considered him from afar for a few minutes before ambling over for a close inspection. Maurice did not reach out to touch the bird, because he knew better. His reward almost certainly would have been a sharp whack on the arm or wrist from a strong, well-aimed flipper.

Some King Penguins in the colony sat hunched, the white-feathered skin of their lower abdomens bulged out and folded over their feet. Each bird was incubating an egg on the feet under the fold of skin. The birds usually sat quite still, but now and again one, murmuring in low tones, leaned over and poked its bill under the fold to examine the egg.

The two King Penguins incubating eggs on the right stand just far enough apart so that they cannot touch each other when they wave their flippers. The birds on the left, probably mates, rest in typical posture.

The only King Penguin egg we actually saw appeared in the mud beside the brook one morning. When we cleaned the egg and placed it in the grass on the edge of the colony, two "unemployed" birds strolled over, examined it carefully, and walked away.

ABOVE, RIGHT AND OPPOSITE
Always on the outskirts of a King Penguin colony are small groups standing for long periods. Perhaps they are birds recently relieved from incubation by their partners and in no hurry to go to sea. Or perhaps "unemployed," they are just killing time until something happens.

LEFT
There are always different stages of the breeding cycle in a King Penguin colony. While some birds are already paired and have eggs, other birds are beginning to pair. Here, a male and female are courting. With lowered heads (top) both penguins open and close their bills rapidly enough to make rattling sounds. Shortly thereafter the male (bottom) arches his neck over the female's and nibbles her gently. Copulation will soon follow. Probably the female will lay her egg on the site where they are courting.

BELOW

Something is happening here. The bird standing tall is about to point its bill skyward and bugle. The bird standing against its chest will do likewise. Then the two birds will begin turning their heads from side to side, flashing their orange ear patches for each other's benefit. Keeping this up, they will walk around strutting with backs arched and chests puffed. Probably these two are a male and female getting acquainted.

The Jackass Penguin comes ashore on the Falkland beaches in the early spring usually in advance of the Gentoos and Rockhoppers. What it lacks in bright colors it makes up for in black-and-white bands on the face and neck and a circle of pinkish skin around the black eyes. The shyest of the penguins in the Falklands, it will, when cornered or blocked in its path, deliver a painful bite by virtue of its sharply hooked bill.

BELOW

Jackass Penguins, like the one on the left, stoop forward when they walk as though favoring a painful kink in the back. When in a hurry or trying to catch up, like the one on the right, they toboggan, skittering on their toes and the tips of their flippers.

Jackass Penguins nest underground in burrows they excavate themselves with bill and claws. In desirable situations, such as soft, peat-covered hillsides or wide sandy flats, their burrows are fairly close together in loose colonies. On this hillside, note the birds sitting on the "doorsteps" of their burrows, all of which overlook the sea.

Announcing itself at the entrance to its burrow, a Jackass Penguin brays like a jackass—hence the origin of the English name for the species in the Falklands. Consisting of a series of doleful sounds decreasing in volume, the whole vocal performance is heart-rending to the human ear.

When we approached Jackass Penguins on their doorsteps, we drew just so near before they turned and ducked into their burrows. But the darkness below was too much for their compelling curiosity and up they soon came just as this bird did. Nearsighted and even less able than most kinds of penguins to see with both eyes straight ahead, the Jackass Penguin cocks and turns the head from side to side to peer first out of one eye and then the other.

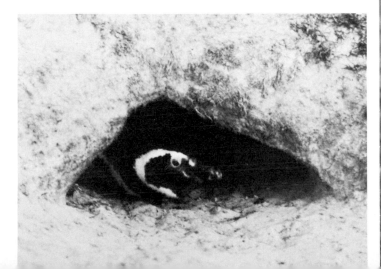

Family portrait on the doorstep. The two young Jackass Penguins, not quite as large as their parents, still have down clinging to the backs of their heads. At this age, they spend more time outside their burrows and frequently venture away short distances.

Like parent, like offspring—in size and posture. Now fully grown, the young bird is nearly independent of parental care and will soon be joining other birds its age and heading for the sea. A year will pass before it looks like the parent and probably three years before it is ready to breed.

Going to sea. Three Jackass Penguins proceed toward the surf. At the right moment they will run and dip into the water receding from a spent breaker and be underway seaward before the next breaker crests.

Parade of the "unemployed." Always in the neighborhood of nesting Jackass Penguins are gatherings of birds, fully adult in appearance, that show no interest in nesting. Most of their time they spend sleeping or endlessly parading.

RIGHT

Where there was an egg under the skinfold of the King Penguin, there is now a chick. For the first few days after birth it stays there and all one can see of it is the head when the parent lifts the skinfold or when the head comes poking out.

BELOW

Whistling faintly for a meal, the chick is obliged by the parent, which bends over, opens the bill slightly, and lets the chick reach in for whatever food the adult has regurgitated.

The time comes when the chick emerges from beneath the covering of feathers and snuggles close to the adult, which tends it constantly, feeding it and gently preening its soft down. Among the neighbors it is an object of interest. The same neighbors will be the first to threaten it should it stray from its parent.

RIGHT

Well fed, the young chick soon becomes very fat with loose wrinkles of skin about the neck. Increasingly, it becomes aware of the world beyond its parent's side and will soon take exploratory steps away although it has difficulty standing on its feet without tottering and will shuffle when it walks.

During the first few weeks the King Penguin chick grows very fast, so fast that before long it no longer fits in the cozy chamber beneath the skinfold. All it can get under cover is the head and shoulders.

BELOW

The chick at this age, about six weeks old, may move away from the parent or the parent may walk away from it—only a short distance. We watched a parent saunter away from one chick this age and could sense real panic in the youngster when it realized it was alone. We could imagine it calling, "Hey! Wait for me," as it hurried to the adult with both flippers waving and tried hard to crawl under the skinfold.

OPPOSITE

After about twelve weeks of age, the young King Penguin is the size of the adult. It has acquired a new coat of down, chocolate-brown in color and so long and soft and fluffy that the chick seems much larger than the adult and looks like a teddy bear.

The King Penguin chick remains in the teddy-bear stage for about seven months, its further development virtually stalled—a unique situation among all species of birds. So slow is the young bird to reach maturity and independence that a pair of King Penguins can rear only two offspring in three years.

After ten months or more of age, the teddy-bear chick begins shedding its down—now faded and somewhat shaggy—from the feet up. The "underwear" gradually revealed is the first generation of mature feathers.

When molting their teddy-bear down, some of the young King Penguins get ahead of the others. The young bird drawing up the rear has shed all of its down except a little remaining on the back of its head and neck.

Two King Penguins bugle. Puffed out up front and pulled in below, backs arched, bills skyward but kept closed, they produce in concert a volley of notes like blasts from a muffled bugle. A teddy-bear chick, belonging to neither yet hopeful for a meal, is ignored.

A meddlesome chick. Two adult King Penguins, a male and a female, were strutting when a hungry teddy-bear chick rushed up to them, whistling for food. Annoyed, both adults dealt the interloper several jabs sufficient to dismiss it. Looking on was another young bird that had shed most of its teddy-bear down.

After all their youngsters have left for the sea and independence, the parent King Penguins stay around or near the colony while they acquire a new covering of feathers. In the process their old feathers come off in patches and litter the landscape. One bird is molting and looks utterly miserable. The other three birds, molting over with, are sleek, shiny, and immaculate in their new feather coats.

Perfect relaxation. Ordinarily, penguins sleep while standing, but here in the warm sun a King Penguin snoozes, flat out.

Part of the New Island colony of nesting Rockhopper Penguins among the pale rocks on the brow of the cliff. The rest of the colony extended over the tops of the cliffs, down into the gullies, and up under the bordering tussock grass. The sound from these small penguins competes in volume with the roar of the Falkland wind. The racket is audible for over a mile on a quiet day.

OPPOSITE

The Rockhopper Penguins often select a site that has a spectacular view. From one part of the New Island colony the nesting birds look down on their landing rock beneath the irregular cliffs—so eroded by wind and waves—and across the tumultuous sea, whose color, as changeable as the Falkland weather, is sparkling turquoise one minute, deep blue the next, and most often a dull steel gray.

Each nest has two eggs which the male and female take turns incubating for about five weeks. While one bird covers the nest, its mate spends most of the time at sea, sometimes for many days.

ABOVE AND OPPOSITE

As far as the eye can see, Rockhopper Penguins on their nests. One wonders how the birds coming back from the sea can remember where their nests are and find them.

This Rockhopper is annoyed about something. When the Rockhopper is disturbed or angry, the black feathers on his head stick straight up and the yellow tufts stick way out.

"I'm here." A Rockhopper, after porpoising in from the sea, hopping and scrambling up the steep trail to the top of the cliffs, then working its way through the colony, now nears its nest and cackles, announcing itself. Its mate at the nest responds similarly and at that the neighbors join in.

"I'm glad you're home." Together at the nest, both partners greet each other in a mutual display that involves bouts of raucous cackling. Although the birds act as though they hated each other, the whole performance is of the friendliest nature, reinforcing the pair bond.

After the pair have celebrated reunion, they settle down to mutual nibbling as though preening each other's plumage. This is a further means of maintaining the bond between them and is kept up until one or the other tires. Eventually, the returning bird takes over the nest, relieving its partner.

If the Rockhopper Penguin relieving its partner at the nest is a female, the male may go about gathering more nesting material. Here a male brings back a blade of tussock grass. Although it will scarcely improve the nest, his mate will accept it and add it to the rim of the nest by bending it and pressing it around her.

ABOVE

Altercation between neighbors. Every now and then a nesting Rockhopper, perhaps to release energy pent up during long hours spent "doing nothing," threatens a nesting neighbor with a jab. The neighbor threatens in return with no further retaliation unless it is irritated. In that case, it grabs the bill of the instigator and a fight ensues, both birds pummeling each other with their flippers until one of them has had enough and pulls away.

LEFT

A few Macaroni Penguins show up in the Falklands. Obviously similar to the Rockhoppers, they differ particularly in the heavier bill with pink corners of the mouth and a golden crest of feathers extending backward from the forehead instead of tufts of yellow feathers emerging from above and back of the eyes.

69

A lone pair of Macaronis nesting among the Rockhoppers. On the island of South Georgia, eight hundred miles east of the Falklands, the Macaronis have colonies of their own in much the same rugged situations. Interlopers here, the Rockhoppers ignore them.

BELOW

A Macaroni Penguin on its nest at right with nesting Rockhoppers for neighbors. Note the closeness of all the nests. Any bird, Macaroni or Rockhopper, that tries to go between these nests is certain to receive jabs and whacks from the sitting birds.

The King Cormorant is the handsomest of all the species of cormorants in the Southern Hemisphere. Both sexes feature a jaunty crest, orange caruncles at the base of the bill, blue-violet skin around the eyes, and a lustrous greenish blue plumage.

King Cormorants nest among Rockhoppers in small colonial enclaves, less often alone as in this picture. Between the King Cormorants and the Rockhoppers there is little contact because the cormorants fly to and from their nests and the Rockhoppers stay far enough away from the cormorants to avoid trouble.

Scattered here and there in the Rockhopper colony are the Black-browed Albatrosses, sitting high on their mud-cone nests. Big birds, they go about their affairs oblivious to the Rockhoppers around them and the Rockhoppers give them slight attention, since the albatrosses, always flying to and from their nests, do not bother them. The albatross nestling, during its first few days, is brooded almost continuously by one parent or the other.

Two Rockhopper chicks, two or three days old, snuggle together close under their parent in a deep nest. One adult stays with the chicks during the day while the other is at sea gathering food—small shrimps, called krill, that float near the surface of the water. At night, both adults are usually together at the nest. Yet despite their constant vigil, a Rockhopper pair rarely raises two young to the age when they are ready to leave the nest.

Aware of our presence, this rapidly growing chick tries to hide under its parent, which spreads its flippers in a defensive pose. By this time, the nest, worn down by trampling feet, has entirely disappeared, yet the pair still claims and occupies the original site.

Mealtime. Both parents mutually display at the nest site upon the arrival of one of them from the sea. As soon as the greeting ceremony is over, the returning parent will oblige its flask-shaped chick with a meal.

The Great Skua, a gull-like bird with hawklike habits, flies slowly over the Rockhopper Penguin colony, searching for an unguarded egg or chick, or a chick that has wandered into a neighboring territory and been killed or hopelessly maimed by the resentful occupants. Nesting penguins, recognizing the predator by the white patches in its wings, sit closer on their eggs or young when it passes over.

A skua devours a penguin chick. Much as we dislike the skua for its depredations, we realize that it helps control the penguin population by culling the weakest chicks. In addition, by taking the carcasses of chicks that have been killed or have died from other causes, the skua serves a sanitary function.

When nearly two weeks old, Rockhopper chicks join others of their age in crèches or nurseries. Here they gain "protection in numbers" from attacks by skuas, and, during cool weather and at night, share their warmth by huddling together. With the formation of the crèches, large sections of the colony, so crowded earlier, are vacant. A few adults linger around the crèches. Once regarded as nursemaids, they are probably unmated birds or birds that have lost their own young.

Below the cliffs in a tidal pool on a sunny day, Rockhoppers—yearling birds, "unemployed" adults, or adults taking a respite from parental responsibilities—bathe and otherwise enjoy themselves by running into the water, swimming a bit, and rushing out.

Swimming underwater in a tidal pool, as here or at sea, the penguin uses its flippers for propulsion just as flying birds use their wings in the air.

Two Rockhopper youngsters, having shed most of their down, are nearly ready to go to sea. Still lacking the red bills and yellow tufts on their heads, they look only remotely like their parents.

LEFT

With no further parental cares, a Rockhopper molts its old feathers. It remains in the colony while the developing new feathers push out the old ones. During its whole molting process the bird must stay ashore and consequently go without food. Its apparent misery is understandable.

BELOW

Dolphin Gulls, such as this one, patrol penguin colonies, searching for any food that an adult may have spilled when feeding its young. Many of the gulls have learned the trick of disturbing and harassing the adult to the point that it inadvertently lets some of the food drop on the ground instead of into the chick's mouth.

After an incubation period of about six weeks, the Gentoo Penguin eggs hatch, though not at the same time. Like all newly hatched birds, the chick retains at the tip of its bill a white "egg tooth" which it used for weakening the shell so that it could get out.

The chicks have coats of short gray down, so thick and soft as to look like plush. Although the chicks appear to be delicate little birds, they are tough from the very start. They have to be, for the parents show slight regard for their feelings and do not mind stepping all over them.

Gentoo Penguins often manage to raise two young, guarding them closely for the first few weeks. One parent is always at the nest, but the chicks, full of energy, occasionally leave its shelter for brief sorties in the immediate vicinity, shuffling back for parental protection at the least sight of a skua overhead or any other sign of danger.

The Gentoo chicks not only grow *up* fast, they grow *out*. This chick fairly bulges, thanks to being well-stuffed with krill, and is content to sit beside the parent. Practically every day, usually in the afternoon, one of the parents returns from the sea with a meal.

On returning from the sea, the Gentoo parent trumpets a series of loud resonant sounds that no bird in the colony can miss hearing. Recognizing the voice of its own parent and expecting food, the hungry offspring, peeping and waving its flippers, shuffles forward to the parent.

All penguins feed their young by a clean, economical method, delicately referred to as regurgitation. The parent bends over and pumps the food, stored in its gullet, into the open mouth of the young bird. Unless the parent and young bird are disturbed during the process, no food falls to the ground and gets dirty and none of it is wasted.

Now approaching the size of the adult and with much of its down shed, the young Gentoo develops an interest in exploring the surroundings of the colony. It stops a moment here and a moment there, examining a rock, a film carton, or any other conspicuous object, then hurrying on to something else. We liked to say it was reaching the "teenage" stage.

When I drew near the colony with my camera equipment, many teenagers came out to inspect me. They pecked at the tripod and scrutinized my boots. Then suddenly, as though deciding that I was just another penguin and not worth further attention, they turned and waddled off to find something really new.

As the nesting season nears the end, the Gentoo teenagers, their down shed and their new feather coats sleek, begin heading for the sea. The adults remain in or near the colony to molt and before long the site of the colony and its surroundings are carpeted with cast-off feathers. Note the windrows of feathers in the foreground, blown from the colony by the wind.

The young Gentoos, along with adults that have yet to molt, head for the sea. On the beach, the youngsters test the water during the day and return to the colony toward evening to receive food from their parents. Eventually, they discover that they can swim and soon learn to capture food. On their own from then on, they spend all their time on the beach or at sea during months to follow.